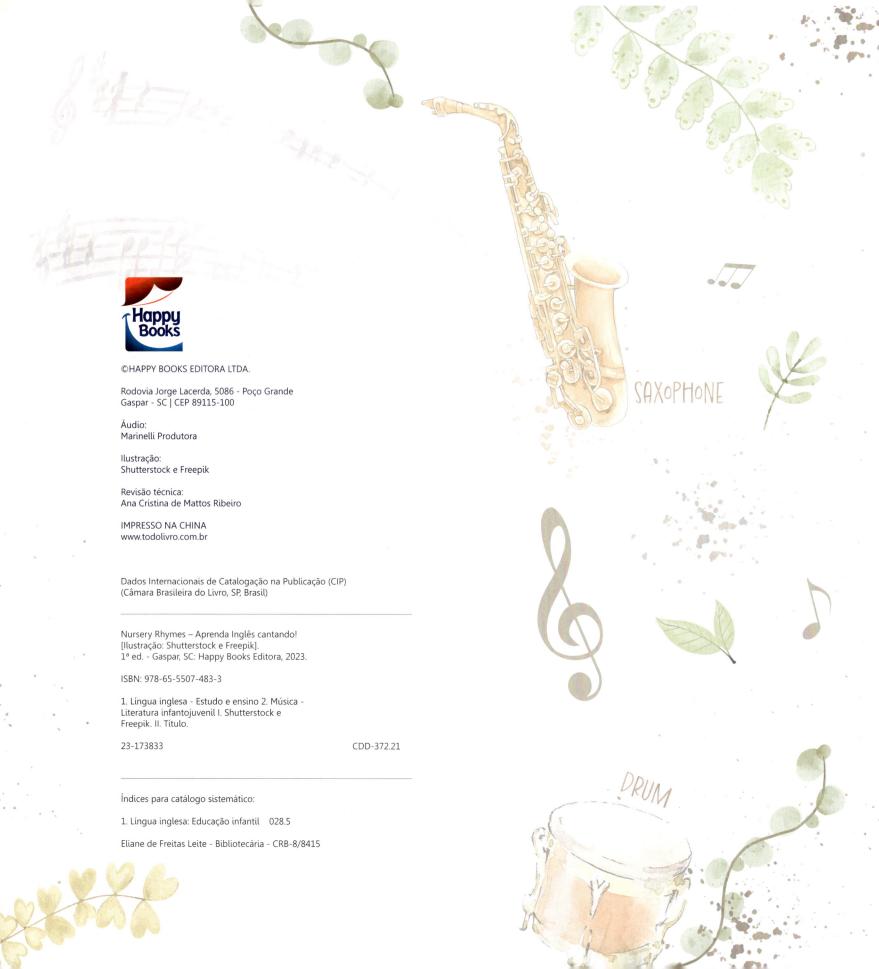

©HAPPY BOOKS EDITORA LTDA.

Rodovia Jorge Lacerda, 5086 - Poço Grande
Gaspar - SC | CEP 89115-100

Áudio:
Marinelli Produtora

Ilustração:
Shutterstock e Freepik

Revisão técnica:
Ana Cristina de Mattos Ribeiro

IMPRESSO NA CHINA
www.todolivro.com.br

Dados Internacionais de Catalogação na Publicação (CIP)
(Câmara Brasileira do Livro, SP, Brasil)

Nursery Rhymes – Aprenda Inglês cantando!
[Ilustração: Shutterstock e Freepik].
1ª ed. - Gaspar, SC: Happy Books Editora, 2023.

ISBN: 978-65-5507-483-3

1. Língua inglesa - Estudo e ensino 2. Música - Literatura infantojuvenil I. Shutterstock e Freepik. II. Título.

23-173833   CDD-372.21

Índices para catálogo sistemático:

1. Língua inglesa: Educação infantil   028.5

Eliane de Freitas Leite - Bibliotecária - CRB-8/8415

Para pais e educadores

A **música** é uma das mais **belas manifestações do espírito humano.** Ocupa lugar de destaque em nossa vida, em diversos momentos e em várias ocasiões. Além de estar sempre tão presente na infância, **contribui para diversos aspectos,** seja por meio de **memórias afetivas,** seja como **instrumento de aprendizado na alfabetização e nas linguagens oral, corporal e verbal;** ajudando a preparar o cérebro para a leitura e a escrita ao desenvolver habilidades de escuta e de atenção, **percepção auditiva do idioma, prática da pronúncia, ritmo e entonação.**

Outro aspecto é com relação ao **estímulo da memória:** à medida que a criança percebe a **velocidade (rápida ou lenta), o volume (alto ou baixo)** e as melodias de uma música, desenvolve a habilidade de distinguir os sons. Conforme essa atividade se repete, ela cria uma memória absolutamente vital para a atividade de leitura. Sendo assim, a introdução ao texto escrito pode ocorrer por meio de canções e rimas. A criança pode reconhecer as letras e tomar consciência de sua estrutura pela música. **Ao aprender músicas recitadas repetidamente, as palavras dessas músicas tendem a fazer parte do vocabulário.** Dessa maneira, a criança aprende a contextualizar **as palavras de uma forma ritmada — o que também ajuda na memorização.**

Nursery Rhymes – Aprenda Inglês cantando é uma coletânea de 32 das mais **belas canções clássicas da língua inglesa para cultivar a tradição e a valorização de uma cultura que atravessa gerações.** Cada canção traz o seu QR CODE e possibilita momentos inesquecíveis de diversão e aprendizado enquanto se está lendo, ouvindo, cantando e apreciando o belo.

Agora que você entende melhor sobre a importância da música,
é só procurar um lugar calmo para vocês curtirem e cantarem juntos!

Para **ouvir**, basta **posicionar a câmera** do seu celular sobre o código.

Sing along with me!

Doctor Foster

Doctor Foster went to Gloucester,
In a shower of rain.
He stepped in a puddle,
Right up to his middle,
And never went there again.

The wheels on the bus

The wheels on the bus go round and round,
Round and round,
Round and round,
The wheels on the bus go round and round,
all day long.

The wipers on the bus go swish, swish, swish
Swish, swish, swish
Swish, swish, swish
The wipers on the bus go swish, swish, swish,
all day long.

The horn on the bus goes beep, beep, beep
Beep, beep, beep
Beep, beep, beep
The horn on the bus goes beep, beep, beep,
all day long.

The children on the bus go up and down,
Up and down,
Up and down.
The children on the bus go up and down,
all day long.

Sing along with me!

Itsy bitsy spider

The itsy bitsy spider
Went up the water spout.

Down came the rain
And washed the spider out.

Out came the sun
And dried up all the rain

And the itsy bitsy spider
Went up the spout again.

Sing along with me!

Sing along with me!

Hickory, dickory, dock

Hickory dickory dock.
The mouse went up the clock.
The clock struck one,
The mouse went down,
Hickory dickory dock.
Tick tock, tick tock, tick tock.

Twinkle, twinkle little star

Twinkle, twinkle, little star,
How I wonder what you are!
Up above the world so high,
Like a diamond in the sky.
Twinkle, twinkle, little star,
How I wonder what you are!

Sing along with me!

Peter, Peter pumpkin eater

Peter, Peter pumpkin eater,
Had a wife but couldn't keep her;
He put her in a pumpkin shell
And there he kept her very well.

Peter, Peter pumpkin eater,
Had another and didn't love her;
Peter learned to read and spell,
And then he loved her very well.

Sing along with me!

Polly Wolly Doodle

Oh, I went down South for to see my Sal,
Sing 'Polly Wolly Doodle' all the day.
My Sal she is a spunky girl,
Sing 'Polly Wolly Doodle' all the day.

Fare thee well, fare thee well,
Fare thee well, my fairy fay.
For I'm goin' to Louisiana for to see my Susyanna,
Sing 'Polly Wolly Doodle' all the day.

Oh, my Sal, she is a maiden fair,
Sing 'Polly Wolly Doodle' all the day.
With curly eyes and laughing hair,
Sing 'Polly Wolly Doodle' all the day.

Fare thee well, fare thee well,
Fare thee well, my fairy fay,
For I'm goin' to Louisiana, for to see my Susyanna,
Sing 'Polly Wolly Doodle' all the day.

Sing along with me!

Sing along with me!

Hey, diddle, diddle

Hey, diddle, diddle,

The cat and the fiddle,

The cow jumped over the moon;

The little dog laughed,

To see such sport,

And the dish ran away with the spoon.

If you're happy and you know it!

If you're happy and you know it, clap your hands!
If you're happy and you know it, clap your hands!
If you're happy and you know it,
And you really want to show it,
If you're happy and you know it, clap your hands!

If you're happy and you know it, stamp your feet!
If you're happy and you know it, stamp your feet!
If you're happy and you know it,
And you really want to show it,
If you're happy and you know it, stamp your feet!

If you're happy and you know it, jump up!
If you're happy and you know it, jump up!
If you're happy and you know it,
And you really want to show it,
If you're happy and you know it, jump up!

If you're happy and you know it, shout "We are!"
If you're happy and you know it, shout "We are!"
If you're happy and you know it,
And you really want to show it,
If you're happy and you know it, shout "We are!"

Sing along with me!

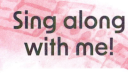

Sing along with me!

Mary, Mary, quite contrary

Mary, Mary, quite contrary,
How does your garden grow?
With silver bells, and cockle shells,
And pretty maids all in a row.

Round and round the garden

Round and round the garden,
Like a teddy bear,
One step, two step,
Tickle you under there.

Sing along with me!

Pussycat, pussycat

Pussycat, pussycat,
Where have you been?
I've been down to London
To visit the queen.
Pussycat, pussycat,
What did you there?
I frightened a little mouse,
Under her chair.

Sing along with me!

The animals went in two by two

The animals went in two by two, Hoorah! Hoorah!
The animals went in two by two, Hoorah! Hoorah!
The animals went in two by two,
The elephant and the kangaroo.
And they all went into the ark,
For to get out of the rain.

The animals went in three by three, Hoorah! Hoorah!
The animals went in three by three, Hoorah! Hoorah!
The animals went in three by three,
The wasp, the ant and the bumblebee.
And they all went into the ark,
For to get out of the rain.

The animals went in four by four, Hoorah! Hoora
The animals went in four by four, Hoorah! Hoora
The animals went in four by four,
The great hippopotamus stuck in the door.
And they all went into the ark,
For to get out of the rain.

The animals went in five by five, Hoorah! Hoorah
The animals went in five by five, Hoorah! Hoorah
The animals went in five by five,
They warmed each other to kept alive.
And they all went into the ark,
For to get out of the rain.

The animals went in six by six, Hoorah! Hoorah!
The animals went in six by six, Hoorah! Hoorah!
The animals went in six by six,
They turned out monkey because of his tricks.
And they all went into the ark,
For to get out of the rain.

The animals went in seven by seven, Hoorah! Hoorah!
The animals went in seven by seven, Hoorah! Hoorah!
The animals went in seven by seven,
The little pig thought he was going to heaven.
And they all went into the ark,
For to get out of the rain.

Sing along with me!

Mary had a little lamb

Mary had a little lamb,
Whose fleece was white as snow;
And everywhere that Mary went,
The lamb was sure to go.

It followed her to school one day,
Which was against the rules;
It made the children laugh and play,
to see a lamb at school.

And so the teacher turned it out,
But still it lingered near,
And waited patiently about
Till Mary did appear.

"Why does the lamb love Mary so?"
The eager children cry;
"Why, Mary loves the lamb, you know"
The teacher did reply.

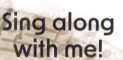

Sing along with me!

Sing along with me!

There was an old woman
who lived in a shoe.
She had so many children,
she didn't know what to do.

She gave them some broth
without any bread;
And whipped them all soundly
and put them to bed.

There was an old woman who lived in a shoe

Sing along with me!

Polly put the kettle on

Polly put the kettle on,
Polly put the kettle on,
Polly put the kettle on,
We'll all have tea.

Susan take it off again,
Susan take it off again,
Susan take it off again,
They've all gone away.

I'm a little teapot

I'm a little teapot, short and stout,
Here is my handle, Here is my spout,
When I get all steamed up hear me shout,
Tip me over and pour me out.

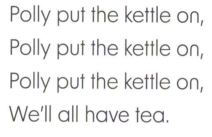
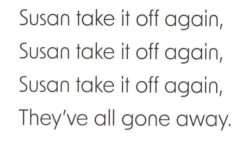

Sing along with me!

Row, row, row your boat

Sing along with me!

Row, row, row your boat,
Gently down the stream,
Merrily, merrily, merrily, merrily,
Life is but a dream...

Row, row, row your boat,
Gently down the stream,
Merrily, merrily, merrily, merrily,
Life is but a dream...

Row, row, row your boat,
Gently down the stream,
Merrily, merrily, merrily, merrily,
Life is but a dream...

Sing a song of sixpence

Sing a song of sixpence,
A pocket full of rye.
Four and twenty blackbirds,
Baked in a pie.

When the pie was opened,
The birds began to sing.
Wasn't that a dainty dish
To set before the king?

Sing along with me!

The king was in his counting house,
Counting out his money.
The queen was in the parlour,
Eating bread and honey.

The maid was in the garden,
Hanging out the clothes,
When down came a blackbird
And pecked off her nose!

She'll be coming round the mountain

She'll be coming 'round the mountain when she comes,
She'll be coming 'round the mountain when she comes,
She'll be coming 'round the mountain,
Coming 'round the mountain,
Coming 'round the mountain when she comes.

She'll be riding six white horses when she comes,
She'll be riding six white horses when she comes,
She'll be riding six white horses,
Riding six white horses,
Riding six white horses when she comes.

And we'll all go out to meet her when she comes,
And we'll all go out to meet her when she comes,
And we'll all go out to meet her,
All go out to meet her,
All go out to meet her when she comes.

She'll be wearing pink pyjamas when she comes,
She'll be wearing pink pyjamas when she comes,
She'll be wearing pink pyjamas,
Wearing pink pyjamas,
Wearing pink pyjamas when she comes.

We'll be singing Hallelujah when she comes,
We'll be singing Hallelujah when she comes,
We'll be singing Hallelujah, singing Hallelujah,
Singing Hallelujah when she comes.

Sing along with me!

Here we go round the mulberry bush

Here we go 'round the mulberry bush,
The mulberry bush, the mulberry bush.
Here we go 'round the mulberry bush,
So early in the morning.

This is the way we wash our clothes,
Wash our clothes, wash our clothes,
This is the way we wash our clothes,
So early Monday morning.

This is the way we iron our clothes,
Iron our clothes, iron our clothes,
This is the way we iron our clothes,
So early Tuesday morning.

This is the way we mend our clothes,
Mend our clothes, mend our clothes,
This is the way we mend our clothes,
So early Wednesday morning.

Sing along with me!

Sing along with me!

Cock a doodle doo

Cock a doodle doo!
My dame has lost her shoe;
My master's lost his fiddling stick,
And doesn't know what to do.

Cock a doodle doo!
My dame has found her shoe;
And master's found his fiddling stick,
Sing doodle doodle doo!

Five little monkeys

Five little monkeys
Jumping on the bed
One fell off
and bumped his head.

Ouch, ouch, ouch
The monkey said.
No more monkeys.
Jumping on the bed.

Four little monkeys
Skipping on the bed
One fell off
and bumped his head.

Ouch, ouch, ouch
The monkey said.
No more monkeys
Skipping on the bed.

Three little monkeys
Running on the bed
One fell off
and bumped his head.

Ouch, ouch, ouch
The monkey said.
No more monkeys
Running on the bed.

Two littte monkeys
Dancing on the bed
One fell off
and bumped his head.

Ouch, ouch, ouch
The monkey said.
No more monkeys
Dancing on the bed.

One little monkey
Spinning on the bed
He fell off
ond bumped his head.

Ouch, ouch, ouch
The monkey said.
Five little monkeys,
Please go to bed!

Sing along with me!

Old MacDonald had a farm

Old MacDonald had a farm (Ee-I-Eee-I-O),
And on that farm, he had a cow (Ee-I-Eee-I-O).
With a MOO-MOO here and a MOO-MOO there,
Here a MOO, there a MOO, everywhere a MOO-MOO.
Old MacDonald had a farm (Ee-I-Eee-I-O).

Old MacDonald had a farm (Ee-I-Eee-I-O),
And on that farm, he had some sheep (Ee-I-Eee-I-O).
With a BAA-BAA here and a BAA-BAA there,
Here a BAA, there a BAA, everywhere a BAA-BAA.
Old MacDonald had a farm (Ee-I-Eee-I-O).

Old MacDonald had a farm (Ee-I-Eee-I-O),
And on that farm, he had a pig (Ee-I-Eee-I-O).
With an OINK-OINK here and an OINK-OINK there,
Here an OINK, there an OINK, everywhere an OINK-OINK.
Old MacDonald had a farm (Ee-I-Eee-I-O).

Old MacDonald had a farm (Ee-I-Eee-I-O),
And on that farm, he had some ducks (Ee-I-Eee-I-O).
With a QUACK-QUACK here and a QUACK-QUACK there,
Here a QUACK, there a QUACK, everywhere a QUACK-QUACK.
Old MacDonald had a farm (Ee-I-Eee-I-O).

Old MacDonald had a farm (Ee-I-Eee-I-O),
And on that farm, he had a horse (Ee-I-Eee-I-O).
With a NEIGH-NEIGH here and a NEIGH-NEIGH there,
Here a NEIGH, there a NEIGH, everywhere a NEIGH-NEIGH.
Old MacDonald had a farm (Ee-I-Eee-I-O).

Sing along with me!

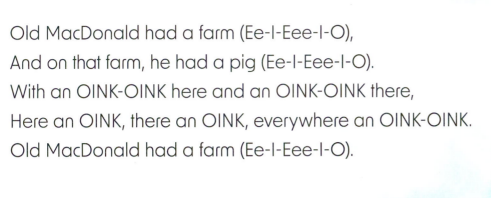

Five little ducks

Five little ducks went swimming one day
Over the hills and far away
Mother duck said, "QUACK, QUACK, QUACK, QUACK,"
but only four little ducks came back...

Four little ducks went swimming one day
Over the hills and far away
Mother duck said, "QUACK, QUACK, QUACK, QUACK,"
but only three little ducks came back...

Three little ducks went swimming one day
Over the hills and far away
Mother duck said, "QUACK, QUACK, QUACK, QUACK,"
but only two little ducks came back…

Two little ducks went swimming one day
Over the hills and far away
Mother duck said, "QUACK, QUACK, QUACK, QUACK,"
but only one little duck came back…

One little duck went swimming one day
Over the hills and far away
Mother duck said, "QUACK, QUACK, QUACK, QUACK,"
and five little ducks came swimming back.

Sing along with me!

A sailor went to sea

A sailor went to sea, sea, sea
To see what he could see, see, see.
But all that he could see, see, see.
Was the bottom of the deep blue
sea, sea, sea!

A sailor went to chop, chop, chop
To see what he could chop, chop, chop
But all that he could chop, chop, chop
Was the bottom of the deep blue
chop, chop, chop!

A sailor went to knee, knee, knee,
To see what he could knee, knee, knee,
But all that he could knee, knee, knee,
Was the bottom of the deep blue
knee, knee, knee!

Sing along with me!

I had a little nut tree

I had a little nut tree,
Nothing would it bear,
But a silver nutmeg
And a golden pear;
The King of Spain's daughter
Came to visit me,
And all for the sake
Of my little nut tree.

Her dress was made of crimson,
Jet black was her hair,
She asked me for my nutmeg
And my golden pear.

I said, So fair a princess
Never did I see,
I'll give you all the fruit
From my little nut tree.

Sing along with me!

One, two, buckle my shoe

One, two, buckle my shoe;
Three, four, knock at the door;
Five, six, pick up sticks;
Seven, eight, lay them straight:
Nine, ten, a big fat hen.

Sing along with me!

Humpty Dumpty

Humpty Dumpty sat on a wall.
Humpty Dumpty had a great fall.
All the king's horses,
And all the king's men,
Couldn't put Humpty together again.

Sing along with me!

One, two, three, four, five
Once I caught a fish alive,
Six, seven, eight, nine, ten,
Then I let it go again.

Why did you let it go?
Because it bit my finger so.
Which finger did it bite?
This little finger on my right.

Sing along with me!

Simple Simon met a pieman

Sing along with me!

Simple Simon met a pieman,
Going to the fair;
Says Simple Simon to the pieman,
Let me taste your ware.

Says the pieman to Simple Simon,
Show me first your penny,
Says Simple Simon to the pieman,
Indeed I have not any.